SOULATRY: POETRY FOR THE SOUL

SOULATRY: POETRY FOR THE SOUL

By Authoress Marion Kay Pittman

So You Can Write Publications[TM]
P.O. Box 80736
Milwaukee, WI 53208
Phone: (920)-821-3006

Published by So You Can Write Publications, LLC
3/7/2021

www.sycwp.com
home4writers@sycwp.com

ISBN: 978-1-6379-0209-7 (sc)

Dedication

This book is dedicated to my amazing, loving, caring, unselfish and patient mother, Lucille Pittman. Who has always encouraged me to tell my story. This book is also dedicated to my grandfather, T. B. Johnson.... I kept my promise.

The Birth

The roars of a million years were in the air the day I was born.

The cries of my people had entered my heart.

The struggle that they had endured had entered my soul.

The sight I was given was for me to see the world, and to do my share in it.

My mouth was there to tell the story of how I become.

My skin was the color of African soil;

My hair was the texture of the people who had walked the African roads before I.

My face was the face of many African Queens and Kings before the world knew that they existed.

My body was built to be strong and steady to conquer any quest that was to be put before me;

and my African children would go through the same rituals as I did, and the many people before me.

Fore we had sat the pace, built the roads that will guarantee our children strength, hope and love;

For one day they shall rule the world.

Take You Back

Take you back to the day,

with backyard barbecues, block parties and kids playing ball in the streets. A game of piggy in the lot, and double Dutch on the sidewalk.

Take you back,

to your uncles and aunts dancing to their favorite songs, and barbecue smoke filled the air. Family all sitting around enjoying each other.

Take you back,

to someone pulling out a deck of cards, checkers and domino's laughing at the loser and congratulate the winner.

Take you back,

to parents asking you to dance for the family, sing for the family, and someone always yelling, "That kid got talent, they got it from me."

Take you back,

to Johnny come across, hopscotch, red light green light, mother may I and Simon says. kids riding their bikes up and down the street.

Take you back,

to marbles, jacks, tic-tac-toe, hang man and building a house out of cards.

Take you back,

to family loving each other, neighbors being a part of your family and a community as one.

Now that takes you back.

I Bid You Farewell

I bid you farewell from years of torture,

I bid you farewell from all the shame.

I bid you farewell from all the lies.

I bid you farewell from all the pain.

I bid you farewell from standing by your side.

I bid you farewell from crying at night.

I bid you farewell to make myself strong,

because you have been unfair to me.

I bid you farewell

because I am finally free; I bid you farewell because I know
that all the torture you've caused me will come back to you.

I do not wish you well.

All I wish for you is a million days in your own personal hell.

Love Fool

I thought I had found true love;

someone that is special to me.

I thought this person would be the answers to my mysteries.

I thought he would come and bring me peace.

I put my heart on the line,

I put my love in his hands.

What was wrong with me?

Why couldn't I see?

Was my love for him one sided?

Were my eyes closed, or were they open and I refused to see?

Doesn't he see how much he mean to me?

Doesn't he realize that I would have walked a thousand miles for him?

But the question is, would he walk a thousand miles for me?

Didn't he realize that I am only human and the pain I would feel would
be real?

I feel like I was given the world to have it taken from me.

Why do I trust?

What is wrong with me?

How can I be a fool?

Why doesn't love, love me?

Where Are They Now? *

Where are the little boys and girls I grew up with?
Where are they now?
Where are the people I use to play with?
Where are they now?
The people I looked forward to seeing every day?
Where are they now?
The people who loved each other as true playmates.
Where are they now?
They now hate each other because they live on different sides of the
street.
They forgot about their true friendships.
They lost each other in hate
Where are the little boys I grew up with?
Where are they now?
Some are doing crime.
Some are doing time.
Some are even underground.
Where are the little boys and girls I grew up with?
Where are they now?

This Man Needs

When I look into his eyes I see my future.

When I look into his heart I see pain.

When I look into his mind I see goals.

When I look, when I look......

This man has so much to conquer.

This man is strong, stronger than he could ever imagine.

This man needs to believe in himself as I do.

This man has a destiny.

This man has a future.

This man needs to let go of his past.

This man needs to start a new.

He needs to learn from his past and embrace his future.

This man needs, this man needs, this man needs......

This man needs nothing because he has it all he just needs to know how to use it!

Does Love, Love You

What to say, when the one that you love treats you that way;
do you run or do you hide?
Do you look for that little safe place inside?
A place where you can run and no one knows where you are,
but what happens when you and your love come face to face?
Do you argue, do you curse, or do you shout and scream all over the
place?
Do you do all those things?
Are you sad that your love used you in such a way?
Are you sad that the love was never here to stay?
Did you stay in a relationship just to have a love by your side?
Did you think that being there for your love would make it right?
Did you think the promises your love made would come true?
If you did, the fool was you...
When will you wake up and see the light that everything you did was not
right.
Your love will never be true to you;
your love would never mean the words, I love you...
your love would only say what it thinks you want it to say. <suggestion>
If your love, loves you it would treat you this way:
your love would come to you with honor and pride,
you love would stand by your side if you were wrong or right,
your love would never lie to you,
your love would never cheat on you,
your love would love you for your inner beauty not just the outer.
If you think that the love you have isn't true,
do what is best for you...
let it go and let true love find you.

Reality

My eyes filled up with tears, knowing that his love for me is gone.

My heart beats to a slower pace knowing that I'm all alone.

<suggestions>

The thought of him loving another makes my body shiver with pain;

for I thought our love was everlasting, that we would be together until the end.

To picture him with another makes my spirit weep;

why did it have to end?

Why do I feel so alone?

Where has all the love gone?

These questions I've asked many times,

the answers I cannot find;

so, I sit and ponder about what was lost,

and all of the pain love has cost.

I wonder whether I can love again, or would I just have special friends.

Prom King 1990

He was Prom King 1990.

He was the most handsome guy you have ever seen,
he stood tall and walked with pride;
he had the most chiseled chin and a dashing smile.
He was Prom King 1990.

He was on all the sports teams,'
he letters in everyone.
Every girl wanted to date him;
every guy wanted to be him.
He was Prom King 1990.

Sixteen years have passed,
and I saw him down at the store;
Prom King 1990.
At first, I didn't recognize him.
He looked so different from before;
he walked with a limp,
his chisel chin was gone,
and the dashing smile wasn't there anymore.
He was Prom King 1990.

His skin was ravished with sores,
his teeth were rotten to the core;
he no longer stood with pride.
He stood at the store asking for spare change,
and I asked him how life had treated him.
He said life had treated him bad.
doing those high school years, he got a habit that took him down.
he started smoking drugs,
then he started sniffing drugs,
and now he is shooting up drugs.
Going in and out of jail.
All of his friends were long gone,

14

All the scholarships he was offered faded away.
No one had time for him,
he wasn't in the limelight anymore.
I wonder what great things he could have become,
but the reality is, that drugs took him down.
As I walked away I looked at him one last time... he was prom king
1990.

Mr. Wonderful

My mystery man, I never knew his name;
all I knew was his game
He played me a whole year long;
just to end with an unspoken song.
What did he see in me?
Why did it end so mysteriously?
Did he ever love me at all?
Was I ever part of the bigger plan...
or was I just a pawn of the mystery man?
He never introduces me to his mother,
he never introduces me to his friends;
or was I just a booty call of the mystery man
To call when he needed a fix,
but why did he pretended to be a wonderful man?
Why did he cater to me?
Why when I was with him, he made me feel free?
What was his goal or what didn't I see?
Did I have my blinders on?
Why did I just let things be?
Did I think he was different?
Did I think he was a part of me?
My mystery man is gone,
my soulmate has sat me free.
My mystery man I loved, but did he ever love me?

The Borrowed Heart

Does his heart belong to me?

Or is it on loan?

When he's with me, is he thinking about her?

When he smiles at me, is he smiling at her?

When he kisses me, does he wish that he could be kissing her?

When he lies beside me at night, does he pretend that I am she?

Is his love for me real or is it make believe?

When he says I love you, is he really saying that he loves her?

Is it me or is it she he loves?

Is it me or she, he wants to spend his time with?

Am I just a toy to past his time away?

Am I just a tool he would use to get her back?

What about my heart?

What about my feelings

What about all the love I have given him?

What about all the sacrifice I've made?

What about it, what about it....what about me?

My Blues Ain't My Own

The blues is a feeling that come from deep down in your soul,
other people can give it to you,
some people say it makes you whole.
It's something that's laying on your chest pressing hard on your bones.
It's something that makes you feel sad and all alone.
It sometimes comes in a song but always in words,
these are thing you don't want to be heard;
my blues ain't my own, I picked them up a long time ago.
I can't get rid of them, it has become a part of my soul.
I carry my blues everywhere I go,
it will not leave me;
it has a tight hold.
My blues ain't my own,
it's other people's problems.
It will not let me free,
it makes me cry,
it makes me weep.
My blues ain't my own, but they are a part of me.

The Gathering

As the morning came the old men gathered under the tree,
each one brought a form of seat with them.
Some brought chairs,
some brought milk crates,
some sat on parked cars;
and other sat on the curb.
These men shared a bottle of whiskey,
passing it from one person to another.
They talked about their families,
they talked about their friends;
they talked about the kind of jobs they had and why those jobs came to
an end.
These men gathered under the tree from sun up to sun down;
each day is the same,
each face never changes.
Each told their life story;
each man shared their pain.
Every day they came to the tree, and laughed, talked and shared bottles
of whiskey with friends.

Friends

We grew up together,
we grew to be the best of friends.
We've smiled,
we've lied,
we've laughed,
and we've cried.
We shared our visions,
we've shared our inner most dreams,
there wasn't a secret that we did not share;
we went everywhere.
You are my buddy, you are my friend;
you were there when I felt alone.
You were there to take my 3:00 am phone call,
you are my buddy, my pal, and my best friend.

Children of Today

Children of today,
Do they laugh and play?
Do they wonder or dream to past their time away?
Can they imagine being grown and on their own?
The answer is no.
The children of today can't laugh, can't play,
because our would have made them that way.
Why should they dream of something that would never be until our
society sat them free?
Children of today have lost their way,
because the parents don't know the meaning of the word stay.
Parents don't nurture,
don't cuddle,
don't say I love you.
They just don't care.
So, what's to say about the children of today?
Take a moment to love the children of today than they would laugh,
play, and imagine their time away.

The Stand

She walks out her door every day,
she always stops in the same place.
She always smiles at her neighbors who pass her way.
She always has a kind word to say,
she stands there night and day.
Her position never changes.
She looks as if she was waiting for someone to come,
she looks as if this person could change her world;
she waits for this person,
she waits night and day.
She never loses the same position,
she always looks the same way.
Maybe one day her mystery person would appear,
maybe one day she would lose her stand.
But until then,
she stands.

My World

Walk into my world
and see what I see;
my world has so much disgust and hate for me.
I can't walk down the street without a total stranger making fun of me.
Why am I hated so much?
What makes me be a target?
Is it because I have more flesh on my bones;
because I am not a size two.
Why can't my world accept me for me?
Why can't I have my dignity?
My world sees me coming and close the door;
my world tells me my prince will not come.
I can't turn on the television without someone telling me to take a pill,
or some person telling me how unhappy they are because they are not thin.
Now the airports are telling me I am too fat to fly and that I have to pay an extra fare.
There are so many people, places, and things telling me not to like me;
they ought to be ashamed, they need to envy me.
I am the epitome of beauty.
I have style, grace and strength that it takes to be a woman of today.
So, go ahead and laugh, and make off the wall jokes,
all that silliness is self-hate.
So, sit back and envy me.

Imaginary Love

She was his imaginary lover.

He built her up to be something she wasn't.

He planned a future for him and her.

He knew his imaginary lover would not lie,

he told her that his love was true.

He knew what the future held for his new-found love.

He looked for her to call him every single day.

He held his breath on every single word that she would say.

He called her his angel that god had sent,

he dreamed one day of becoming husband and wife;

and be a father to rise his children right.

He was the one who confess his love every night,

his eyes were filled with love, and so was his heart.

He knew that he had done something right and that God had smiled on him.

Although he confesses his love, he thought his love was true.

He knew that if he showed her to the world all the world would have knew.

That his imaginary love was not perfect and that the world would have known,

but she was unique,

but he still loved her truly,

but he made an awful mistake;

he let the world chose who he could love.

He decided to set her free.

He lost out on a true love,

he lost out on a true friend;

he lost out on his soul mate.

He let the world choose his destiny,

so, now he must live with his lost.

Queen for a Day

There once was a girl, and Angel was her name.

She laughed, she played, and she daydreamed her time away.

she would dream that she could be Queen for just one day;

she would take all the guns away and melt them down to make toys for the children of the world could play.

She would end all the wars with a twinkle of an eye.

She would make everyone so happy, just happy to be alive.

There would be no hunger and all the illness would disappear.

It is very sad to say that all angel's dreams came to an end on that very day.

As angel sat on her front stairs daydreaming her time away,

a man ran up to her and grabbed her and put her in the air.

Bullets like airplanes came flying through the air,

he used angel for a shield and then dropped her to the ground.

Angel lay there with no life in her eyes;

her mother wished it could have been her who died.

If only angel could have lived to be Queen for just one day,

we would have a safe and peaceful world for the children to play.

Jane Doe

She walks down the street,
she doesn't know where she is going;
she walks with her head hanging low,
she walks so she can see the ground.
She searches for drugs,
she is looking for that quick high.
She has six children and they all are in the system.
She had a dream of being a fashion model,
she had a dream about being a star;
she would tour the world.
Everyone would love her.
Her face would be on magazine and tv ads,
her name would be on all the top designers' lips.
As she walks down the street she passes a mirror,
she takes a long look at herself;
she is now skin and bones.
She remembered how her skin used to glisten in the sun;
she remembered how men used to complement her on her body.
Now people pass her by or even walk on the other side of the street.
Her life is at a standstill.
Her family disowned her,
her friends are just like her.
So, she walks the street and searches for drugs,
her life exists only to find the next high.
When will her struggle end?
She came across this guy and he was given drugs away for free.
She thought she had hit the lottery!
She ran to a vacant lot and took the gift that the stranger gave,
she no longer has to look for another high.
The dream of being a fashion model was dead.
No one would remember her name;
her family would never know that she was dead.
No one would even care.
The coroner will come by and pronounce her dead;

26

then he will and scoop her up and place her in a pauper's grave.
No lavish funeral or even a song of praise;
the drug took her dreams and now it has taken her life.
The unknown person jane doe is dead.

Inner City Lockdown

Concrete walls, concrete halls;
children running the streets all day and night
no parents in sight.
Drug dealers on the prowl,
looking for the young.
Drug users so high they don't know where they belong.
Inner city lockdown, what you want they have;
abandon buildings, vacant lots and empty schools that isn't fair.
People putting their body up for sale,
city buses $2.00 a fare, if you had a job you could not get there.
Children dodging bullets, drugs and pedophile's just to go to school.
Condo's $124,000 to start where the housing projects use to be.
Inner city lockdown makes Dow Jones sore,
crime is big business.
The more crime the more state money fills the man's pocket.
The more the man's pocket is filled, the less the community see.
The people can't pay their taxes and they lose their homes.
Organizations that can't meet their status quo and shut their doors.
Big businesses purchase up the vacant lots and foreclosed homes.
You can't afford to live in your neighborhood.
Now what do you do when inner city lockdown comes after you?
Arm yourself with knowledge, know your rights;
turn this all around and make it right.
Make your school system strong, and chase drug dealers away.
Get the drug users some help and send them on the right way
Turn the inner-city lockdown to inner city prosperity.

Girls vs. Girl

There she goes,
she thinks she is so fine;
We will teach her not to mess with anything of mine.
James is my man and she is wasting our time.
Let's get her, girls it's time.
As the girls walked toward her they begin to pull out their weapons.
"Hey you," the girls yelled.
As the girl turned around, hit, hit, cuts and several kicks,
the girl fell to the ground.
The girl never knew what happen,
she never had a chance to wonder why.
She will never have a prom or a wedding day;
she will never enjoy another sunny day,
her life ended on that day.
As the girls gathered around her and laughed,
the police sirens filled the air.
The girls begin to run,
and one by one the girls were captured.
One by one the girls were prosecuted,
one by one the girls got sentenced.
One by one lost them
girls vs. girl.
Now, what was that all about?

Chivalry is Dead

I went to a funeral no women ever want to attend.

There, lying in the casket was every women's friend.

It has been their friend from the beginning of time.

This friend made women feel special,

this friend separated the boys from the men.

This friend death marked the beginning of the end.

No longer would men give up their seat,

no longer would men tip their hats,

no longer would men not use foul words in the presence of women.

No longer would men pull out your chair.

Chivalry is dead and it lying up there;

so, when you're walking down the street with heavy bags in your hands,

keep on walking girl because these men would not lend a hand.

Or when you see an elderly lady get on a crowded bus no man would stand.

She's out of luck.

So, ladies just give in,

chivalry is dead and would never come back again.

Gone are the days when a total stranger made you feel special just because you are a woman.

So, let's remember chivalry in his finest days

and thank him for the kind words and gestures he made.

Chivalry is dead and he won't be back.

So, ladies let's all stand and say goodbye to the last honorable man.

He Loved Me

He loved me, hell, I know he does;
he pays my rent,
he buys me clothes.
He takes me to the finest restaurants,
he takes me to the hottest shows,
he makes sure all my bills are paid.
He makes sure all of his feelings for me are known.
He takes me to work and picks me up too.
So, what if I have a few bruises,
they don't always show.
It's only a few minutes of pain and no one ever knows.
So, what if I cry and beg for my life.
So, what he throws me to the floor,
because he says that is the only way I would learn to act right.
He loves me and this I know;
his love for me will last me a lifetime because he told me so.
Too bad I will never love another.
Today they are closing my casket and lowering it into the ground,
all my bills got paid
and my rent was never late.
I had the most stylish clothes that they put on me as they laid me to
rest,
everything I thought meant the world to me.
He loves me and this I know;
he loved me so much that I lay dead and will never love no more.
I wish that I had never taken those things he gave me,
I wish after the first hit I let him go.
I wish for so many things that I couldn't wish for anymore.
My life is over and his love for me has brought it to an end,
he who took my life was my lover and my friend.

The Unexpected

Standing at the bus stop watching the cars go by,
wondering when will my bus come and why is it taking so long.
Just when I think my day is starting out wrong, that's when the
unexpected came along.
I wonder who this guy is and what does he really wants?
He seems to be a pleasant guy, this I saw that in his eyes.
So, when he asked me for my phone number I oblige,
taking a chance, I haven't taken in so long.
I gave him my number and waited by the phone,
he called me with a sincere voice, and we talked very long time.
He even found time to call me when he was far from home,
and when his phone broke, I thought the calls would end;
but when that happen that didn't stop him.
I can describe him as an intelligent guy with great hopes and dreams,
living a life with pride and great esteem;
and when he kissed me, he made my spirit float.
His words are sincere, I can tell in his voice;
he has a lot of patience for me and makes me say what is really on my
mind.
I am a little timid at times;
I think he is a sweet guy and I would like to spend a lot more time with
him,
but I know wonderful things take time.
So, to that wonderful guy I met waiting for the bus,
one day we will not be so busy and we can finally hook up.

* Ghetto Girl *

Ghetto girl here she comes,
with her hair in braids,
with her designer jeans, shirt, jacket and boots on.
With attitude she walks,
with attitude she talks;
the girl got game,
the girl is street smart.
Every day you may see her,
Every day you may think that she is a girl from the street.
You may think that she doesn't have a dream or a goal.
You make think that she drinks, or hell, that she even smokes.
You may think that you can see her future of unwanted pregnancies,
public assistance, a rap sheet, a drug habit, or an STD.
are you seeing the same girl I see?
I see a young lady full of life,
I see a young lady full of dreams.
I see her going to school every day, with her backpack on her back.
I see a future lawyer or a doctor, a person with unlimited possibilities.
I see a successful woman who would never forget where she came
from.
be careful not to judge, when you see a girl that may live in a place that
you call a ghetto.
Look at her just as a person like you,
and embrace that girl because you will be embracing your future.

The Inner Child

Hope is my name.

I linger in everyone minds;
I am the key in everyone's soul.
I am the dreams that everyone dreams;'
I am your today and tomorrow.
I can get you through your darkest hours,
I can get you through your saddest days.
You are all a part of me,
because I am a part of you.
I never get frustrated for I know there is a better way.
It might take time but, I know you will make it.
I am inside of everyone,
but sometimes they don't know if I exist.
But once they discover me and set me free,
they can achieve and maintain anything they can imagine.

The Shadow of a Child

The shadow of a child,
so tall so clear;
not fearing anything that comes near.
The shadow of a child, knows no color or skin,
no hatred or hurt within.
A shadow of a child is where we all begin,
so new so pure and so much love within.
It is only when the shadow fades away;
no more laughter,
no more love,
nothing but tears and hate.

In Search of Man

Man was molded from the earth,
to be independent and strong.
God gave him the shape of his own;
to be a leader,
to be a survivor.
He was made to be the protector of life.
He was placed on earth to be the leader of his family.
He was to care for the world;
he is man, husband, father, brother and a true companion.
Man, where are you?
You have left us all alone.
Who does the family look too?
Women are raising your children alone,
but we have faith.
We know that God would lead you back home,
your family is reaching out to you.
The future of man is being destroyed,
man, where are you?
Come back where you belong.

The Gift

It was left on my doorstep,
no return address was on it.
It had my name on the label.
It wasn't wrapped in the finest of paper,
it didn't have a big fancy bow.
It wasn't in a large box
this I know,
it didn't come by UPS or FED-EX.
It didn't come from the post office;
what is up with this?
On the label it reads, "The gift that keeps on given,"
and that it was indestructible.
But if it shall fall it would break?
But once you pick it up and believe it would come back together again.
What kind of gift is this?
Why was it given to someone like me?
What made me so special?
Has this gift been given to another?
As I stood there on my front porch, an angel appeared before me and
said,
"He gives you the gift of life,
though sometimes you may fall.
But if you have faith in him, you will always get up,
you are built to last."
You are here for a reason.
you have so much self-worth, and he would never leave you.
So, take this gift and carry it everywhere you go,
and pass it on to someone you know.
Let them know it is the gift that keeps on given
because God said so.

The Keys

Little kids playing games and dancing in the sun;
pretending and singing all their childhood songs.
Enjoying life and being so young;
living every moment in the sun.
A child smile is worth a million of suns,
to see them dancing and singing the whole day long.
Pretending to be something that they are not,
and having so much fun is what childhood is all about.
Laughing and running just for fun,
to make childhood memories.
To live out dreams,
to make history.
Little kids playing and dancing in the sun;
they are the keys to our future.
They are the hope for our survival;
the world is at their feet.
So many wonders and adventures are waiting for them;
so many new things that they will do and see.
Little kids playing and dancing in the sun.

Fat Girl

Look at her,
look how fat she is.
She would be so pretty if she was thin.
Statistics says she will never go to college,
statistics says she will never get a job,
statistics says she will never have kids.
The fat girl looked up at them and said,
"What kind of world you live in,
I am fat and I am fine,
and I possess of all this beauty and yes, it is all mine."
Beauty is when I go to sleep,
beauty is when I brush my teeth;
all this beauty you see is every ounce of me.
And as far as college goes, I have my degree,
what do you have?
Let me see.
Yes, I have been married and hell, I've been divorced too,
and I have put in my 9 to 5 for over ten years.
Oh, yes, about the kids, I guess god did the immaculate conception
thing again.
Here are my beautiful children holding hands,
stereotypes are all you know.
Stereotypes will not make you grow.
So, look at this fine example before you, and shut your pie hole!

You People Want What

What, you say you want reparations?

Reparations for what?

Don't you know we gave you a ride on our big boats?

You didn't have to pay a thing,

the trip was free,

the price you say is due is now on me?

We gave you a job seven days a week,

we gave you free room and board, and all the leftovers you could eat.

Now, you want reparations?

We let you raise our families,

we let you grow our farms;

we let you people clean our house and cook our food.

Now, you all say reparations is due?

No, I think that reparations have been done.

So, what you built this nation off the sweat off your backs;

we run this nation and that is a fact!

Reparations now, you mean reparations never.

So, you can scream and you all can shout;

so, go ahead and march on Washington and tell them what this is about,

but little did they know we African American people was right.

You stole us from our land,

you stole our history; you made us work for free,

you stole our dignity.

You abused our bodies,

you solid our minds;

you did the worst kind of rape of mankind

and now you don't want to pay?

It is too late mister, you have had your day.

Reparations now and let us be.

Free to help ourselves and our communities.

Free to say justice was due.

Free to let the world know all the heartache you have put us through.

Reparations now! Reparations now! Reparations now!

The Unknown

In the darkest of night, there is always a light.
On the cloudiest of days, there is always a ray of sunlight.
In a world that has war, you can always find peace.
In a nice place I would rather be;
a safe place for me.
Without the lies,
without the distrust,
without the cries I hear so much;
wondering what my day would be like.
Hoping and wishing that my day would turn out right.
Seeking and feeling the unknown;
knowing the place that I belong.

The Watchers

Can't turn on the TV,
they are looking.
can't turn on the radio,
they are listening
you can forget the computer,
they saw you when you bought it.
They are watching when you drive down the street,
they are watching you while you sleep.
Whatever happen to the land of the free, and the promise of peace and
serenity?
Who is watching me?
In this great world of technology privacy is no longer free.
Should I have to buy my privacy
You know everything about me;
where I work,
where I go to school,
where I shop,
what I eat.
And who I am in a relationship with;
you know my medical history.
You know too much about me,
yet I know nothing about you.
What kind of life do you live?
What do you like to do?
Why are you watching me?
I heard people say, it is for my wellbeing and my happiness,
but is that true?
I believe you're watching me to know all my secrecy, my dreams and all
my fantasies;
but who are watching you?

The Sun

When the morning comes,
it is the first thing to take its place.
It is the first thing you see.
It brings warmth and glow to all of us.
It shines all over the place;
it is the bringer of life.
It leads you out of darkness and into the light.
It feeds us all: human, animals, and plants.
It shines without praise.
It is always on time and never late.
So, take advantage of this gift.
The gift of the sun.

Represent

Knowledge, she possesses with style and grace,
passion she has for the human race.
Love, she gives unconditional and strong
Patience she gives is lifetime long
She sees with her heart and not with her eyes
She's a grandmother, mother, sister, aunt; she is the epitome of pride.
What a wonderful creature God has made.
To walk among the human race;
a nurturer from birth.
To stand strong by her man;
she is a survivor.
She understands;
she knows the key to be a woman.

In My Dreams

In my dreams,
I see a man with style and grace.
With strong features any woman wants to embrace.
I see a man that is very intelligent and also, wise;
that does his job with pride.
He is the epitome of man and I want to be by his side.
He is warm, passionate and when he touches me he makes me shiver.
In my dreams, I saw your face,
I see our future,
I saw my soulmate.

Granddaddy's Heart

When I think of my grandfather,
I smile.
I think about all the wonderful things we did,
I smile.
I think about the long talks and walks we had,
I smile.
I think about the songs we sang,
I smile.
I think about all the sports we used to watch together,
I smile.
I think about the life long lessons he taught me,
I smile.
When I think about him, I smile.
He made me feel special;
he helped me develop into a strong person.
He made me love life.
He opened up a new world for me.
He let me enjoy every second of being a child,
and for that, I will always smile.

Secret Keeper

If I tell you a secret, you promise to not to say a word?
You can't tell anybody, you have to hold it to your soul.
Only the four of us will know;
you, me, him and God.
It is a secret of what happens to me every other night.
When my sweet and charming husband comes home,
when he has had a rough day
he sometimes yells and shouts.
That is on a good day,
but when my sweet and charming husband comes home and he has had
a bad day
he slaps me, punches me, kicks me and throws me on the floor.
He calls me out of my name and some names I don't even know.
He tells me I deserve it with every single blow.
My sweet and charming husband, I don't know him anymore.
He takes care of me to the fullest definition of the word,
but you can't tell anyone, not one soul.
My sweet and charming husband is the pillar of this community.
His power reaches very far,
and I am afraid if it gets out, he would not love me anymore.
So, I have told you my secret and you promise to hold it to your soul.
So, if anything ever happens to me at least you will know.

Acknowledgements

First, I would like to acknowledge my amazing, loving, caring, unselfish and patient mother, Lucile Pittman. Secondly, I would like to acknowledge my grandfather T.B. Johnson, who has always encouraged me to be myself and to be a published author. Granddaddy I kept my promise! Thirdly, I would like to acknowledge my two son, Howard Guyton and Xaiver Guyton for the joy they bring to my life. Fourthly, I would like to acknowledge my siblings who were my first audience. I would also like to thank author and founder of So You Can Write Publications, LLC Author Kendrick Watkins for taking that phone call from a person who has given up hope of becoming an author. Last but certainly not least, Authoress Clara Fleming who took me under her wings and gave me encouragement and guidance. I thank you.

Made in the USA
Las Vegas, NV
20 September 2021